OWED

ALSO BY JOSHUA BENNETT

The Sobbing School

OWED

Joshua Bennett

PENGUIN POETS

PENGUIN BOOKS

An imprint of Penguin Random House LLC
penguinrandomhouse.com

LIBRARY OF CONGRESS CATALOGING-IN-PUBLICATION DATA

Names: Bennett, Joshua (Poet), author.
Title: Owed / Joshua Bennett.
Description: New York : Penguin, [2020] |
Series: Penguin poets |
Identifiers: LCCN 2020005147 (print) | LCCN 2020005148 (ebook) |
ISBN 9780143133858 (paperback) | ISBN 9780525505655 (ebook)
Subjects: LCGFT: Poetry.
Classification: LCC PS3602.E664483 O94 2020 (print) |
LCC PS3602.E664483 (ebook) | DDC 811/.6—dc23
LC record available at https://lccn.loc.gov/2020005147
LC ebook record available at https://lccn.loc.gov/2020005148

Printed in the United States of America

Set in Dante MT Std
Designed by Ginger Legato

For the unheralded

ACKNOWLEDGMENTS

Sincerest thanks to the following journals for publishing earlier versions of the work featured in this collection:

African American Poetry: 250 Years of Struggle and Song: "America Will Be"

The American Poetry Review: "Metal Poem," "Mike Brown Is a Type of Christ," and "When Thy King Was a Boy"

The Best American Poetry 2019: "America Will Be"

Boston Review: "Elegy for Prison," "Frederick Douglass Is Dead," and "Owed to Long Johns"

Catch & Release: "Palimpsestina"

Connotation Press: "Elegy for the Modern School" and "The Open"

The Cortland Review: "Purple City Byrd Gang"

The Journal: "Owed to Ankle Weights" and "Token Sings the Blues"

The Kenyon Review: "Owed to Your Father's Gold Chain"

The New York Times Magazine: "The Panther Is a Virtual Animal"

PEN America: "Elegy for the Police State"

Poetry: "The Book of Mycah," "Owed to Pedagogy," and "Reparation"

Public Pool: "Owed to the Durag"

Smartish Pace: "You Are So Articulate with Your Hands"

Soul Sister Review: A Poetry Compilation: "Barber Song"

Storyscape: "Owed to the High-Top Fade"

Transition: "Owed to the 99 Cent Store"

Wave Composition: "Plural"

wildness: "Summer Job"

World Literature Today: "Still Life with Toy Gun"

Thank you, first and foremost, to my family: my late grandmother, Charlotte Elizabeth Ballard, my mother, my sisters and brothers, nieces and nephews, and my father, with whom I share the cover image adorning this book. Thank you to my editor, Paul Slovak, for agreeing to go on this adventure with me yet again. Thank you to my friends, students, mentors, and collaborators, for the constant reminders that this work is worth doing: Thomas Alston, Jamil Baldwin, Kyle Brooks, Jamall Calloway, Devin Chamberlain, Daniel Claro, Ben Crossan, Aracelis Girmay, Jarvis Givens, Bill Gleason, *Carlos Andrés Gómez*, Marc Lamont Hill, Elleza Kelley, Carvens Lissaint, Jesse McCarthy, Roshad Meeks, Ernie Mitchell, Wesley Morris, Nicholas Nichols, Imani Perry, Timothy Pantoja, Gregory Pardlo, Samora Pinderhughes, Justin Reilly, Caroline Rothstein, Elaine Scarry, Josef Sorett, Daniella Toosie-Watson, Jachele Velez, Bee Walker, Rog Walker, and L. Lamar Wilson.

Sincerest thanks to Cave Canem for serving as home and harbor for a number of these poems before they were published. Thank you, as well, to the National Endowment for the Arts, the Society of Fellows at Harvard University, and the Department of English and Creative Writing at Dartmouth College for the various forms of institutional support that helped make this manuscript possible.

Finally, I want to thank my beloved, Pam, for being a friend to my mind. And making every day shine.

CONTENTS

III.

We are a nation within a nation, a captive nation within a nation.

—James Baldwin

Their country is a Nation on no map.

—Gwendolyn Brooks

It is not down on any map; true places never are.

—Herman Melville

TOKEN SINGS THE BLUES

You always or almost
always only one
in the room
Maybe two
Three is a crowd
Three is a gang
Three is a company
of thieves   Three is
wow there's so many of you
Three will get you confused
with people that look nothing
like you you get called
Devin your name isn't
Devin you do your best
not to ignore such casual
erasure you know silence
will be received as affirmation
praise even & you always affirmative
You affirmative action action figure
You fantastic first black
friend   You first-ballot
quota keeper   You almost
cry when your history
professor says *you know*
in this country the gold standard
used to be people Funny how
no one comes right out
& says things like *you people*
anymore it's all code
words like *thug* or
diversity hire You diversity
all by yourself   You contain
multitudes & are yet
contained everywhere you go
confined like there is always

someone watching you & isn't
there & isn't that the entire point
of this flesh you inherited
this unrepentant stain be
twice as good mama says
as if what they have is worth
your panic worth measuring
your very life against & you always
remember to measure
Your hair, your volume, your tone
over email, you perpetually
sorry   You don't know why
You apologize to no one
in particular just for being around
& in your body at the same time
You know your body
is the real problem
You monster   You beast
of burden You beast & burden
You horse but human
You centaur You map
the stars & pull back your bow
to shoot
          the moon in its one good white eye

You are everything

your big sister says
& on your best
days above ground you
believe her

OWED TO PEDAGOGY

for 1995

It was the dead center of summer,
& anyone but us would've been
outside hours ago, flailing

like a system of larks against
the hydrant's icy spray. But a girl
had her orders, & to disobey

our mother was, in a sense, to invite
one's own destruction, cause to pray
that a god of mercy might strike first.

So we lay, still as stars on the living
room floor, poring over formulae:
divisors & dividends, *quotient*

the first synonym for resolution
I ever learned, & would later
come to love for its sound alone,

how it reminded me, even then,
of words like *quantum* & *quotation
mark*, both ways of saying nothing

means what you think it means
all the time. The observable
universe hides behind its smooth

obsidian dress, & all we can
do is grasp at it in myths
& figures, see what sticks,

give all our best language
to the void. What dark irony,
these coy, child philosophers,

theorizing how things break
from the floor of a house
where everything is more

or less in flux, indeterminate
as the color of the blood
in a body. Or the speed

at which I learned
to obliterate the distance
between myself

& any given boy
on the block, the optimal
angle of the swing

most likely to drop
another kid cold
in front of his crew,

to square up, square
off, & this too was a kind
of education, the way

my sister held both fists
semi-adjacent, each an inch
or so from her switch

-blade eyes, showed me
the stance you take
when the math doesn't

quite shake out, so it's just
you & the unknowns
& the unknowns

never win.

THE BOOK OF MYCAH

Son of Man. Son of Marvin & Tallulah. Son of Flatbush & roti & dollar
vans bolting down the avenue after six. The boy grew like a debt, &
beautified every meter of the pockmarked, jet-black asphalt which
held him aloft on days he sped from much larger men along its skin.
Godfathers & hustlers, Division I scholarship forfeiters, alchemists,
liars, lasagna connoisseurs, internet mixtape DJs & baby mama
conflict consultants, each one appearing as if from the smoke of our
collective imagination, Jordans laced, drawstrings taut, all of them
gathered one by one to race the gangly, mop-top prodigy from the
front of Superior Market to the block's endarkened terminus, the same
corner where Man Man got jumped so bad at the back end of last
summer, neighborhood residents came to regard the place as a kind of
memorial & it was like this every other afternoon, you know, from
June through the final days leading up to the book drives & raucous
cookouts which signaled our school year's inauspicious return. This
was the manner by which Mycah Dudley first gained his fame, dusting
grown men without so much as the faintest scintillation of sweat to
make the performance ethical. It was damn near unsportsmanlike, his
effortlessness, mass cruelty in a New York City dreamscape, the
laughter of girls with hip-length, straight-back braids & baby powder
Forces making every contest an event worth leaving the perch of your
bunk bed, stepping out into the record-breaking swelter that summer
held like a trapdoor for kids with broken box fans & no mother home
for at least four more hours to fill the quiet with discipline.

::::

We gathered in swarms to gawk at our boy before takeoff. His flesh
maroon-clad from head to foot like an homage to blood, black plastic
afro pick with a fist for a handle jutting from the left side of his high-
top fade, his high-top Chuck Taylors, size 12, sounding like ox hooves
once he entered the groove of a good run & the distinction was
basically moot at that point is what I am saying, the line between
him & any other mystical creature, any worthwhile myth, any god of
prey or waning life.

:::

The entire block was out that night. Firecrackers packed the
blackening air, their fury matched only by the exorbitance of dope
boy convertibles turned mobile dancehalls by the moment's weight.
Which might explain why no one quite remembers when, or how,
the now-infamous brawl began. Only that Mycah was in rare form
earlier that evening, having just embarrassed Mars Patterson—so
named, it bears mentioning, for the chocolate bars he loved to steal &
trade on the 4 train, not the red rock planet or lord of war—but was
now in his everyday mode, seated on the stoop, a seer with so few
words for devotees & passersby, each eventually stopped asking for
his backstory, for his praise or functional wisdom, & instead were
content to let him eat his veggie patty with cheese without
interruption, which he did, which he was, when the din that always
accompanies someone's son's public pummeling rang out, cut
through our scene lengthwise, compelled the boy, for the first time
on record, to leap from the steps of the brownstone his nana died
braiding hair inside of, enter the scrum, thresh the crowd for signs of
the conflict's center.

:::

General consensus has it he was looking for his little cousin, & found
him, even before the initial cop car ran like a living ram through the
people. Before the boys in blue sprang, a spray of navy fléchettes,
from behind its doors. Before they were caught in the scuffle,
released ten to twenty rounds of ammo into the crowd without
warning, bullets glancing off of Cutlass doors & corner store glass
built for battle, all but three or four of which entered the boy
mid-stride, lifted his six-foot frame from the ground, legs still pumping.
For a second, you would almost swear he was running *through* the
gunfire, preparing for liftoff or something, little cousin held firmly in
his arms, shielded from the onslaught. *They never would have caught
him if he hadn't been holding that child*, said no one, though we all
thought it during the weeks following that moment we each froze,
the moment his body collapsed slow as petals upon the unremarkable

cement, & we stared at our champion felled by an outcome so common we don't even have a special name for it. Still. No one standing ran that day. Most of us turned to face his killers, hands at our sides, determined to make them make it a massacre. But all that was before we heard Man Man let off a scream so full it rent the crowd in two, split the circle we had built around the boy's corpse, our human wall parting to watch each casing fall from Mycah's still-wet, dark-red sweatshirt onto the street. Hear me. I heard the gunman's greeting. Saw hollow points etch apertures into the boy's clothes. They shot Mycah Dudley, quite legally. He died that night. He rose.

BARBER SONG

Postmodern blackness black
-smith. Straight razor reshaping
self-esteem. You dream

in geometries unreachable
by any other means. Speak,
& entire phrases abandon

Standard American
Etymology; hence, you liberate
waves from the sea, *cornrows*

from the cornfield, reclaim *fade*
so I now hear the word & imagine
only abundance, *Caesar*

never meant anything to me
but a cut so close you could see
the shimmer of a man's thinking.

You are how we first learn
to bend language built
to unmake us, accept

implausible risk: some
much older man,
shaver in hand

like a baton full of wasps'
gossip, asking *with the grain
or against* & the question feels

damn near existential
given this is the only
place we can live

in such thoughtless proximity
to another person's open
hands, be held by the face,

ask outright to be made
glamorous, shaped
by your polymathic

brilliance. You biweekly
psychoanalyst, first stop
before funeral, before

wedding & block party
alike, you soothe
-sayer, cooing children

to calm as they sit
in the chair for the first
time, as still a storm

as one might reasonably
expect, you ethicist, defending
hairlines at all cost, your vigilance

keeping online & otherwise
slander at bay. Philosopher king.
Thesaurus in the drawer,

dominoes & scotch & Barbasol
adorning your countertop,
right above the chorus

line of clippers swaying
to the clamor of checkmates
& offhand insults now filling

the shop, each moving
as if the unfettered
locks of some great

metal monster, some faraway
watcher, & you, guardian
of it all. Clean as a pope.

OWED TO THE DURAG

Which I spell that way because that's the way it was spelled
on all the clear plastic packets I grew up buying for no more
than two dollars, two fifty max, unless I was at Duane Reade
or some likewise corporatized venue but who buys
the majority of their durags at Duane Reade anyway,
who would actually wage war on the durag's good name
by spelling it *d-e-w* hyphen *r-a-g*, as I recently read
some sad lost souls do in an article in *The Guardian*?
This isn't botany. This isn't a device one might use
to attend to the suburban garden & its unremarkable
flora, drying freshly damp wisteria with black silk
or the much more common nylon-rayon-cotton blend.
I could see *d-o* hyphen *r-a-g*. That works for me.
One could argue this version makes more sense
even than the spelling I am accustomed to,
reflective as it is of nothing other than itself.
I have never heard the term *do* used in a sentence
by anyone other than a long-lost colleague
at Princeton who once reached wide-eyed
for my high-top fade before a swift rebuke,
marked by my striking his wrist as if some large
though distinctly nonlethal mosquito, surely a top six
proudest moment of anticolonial choreography
I have dared call mine in this odd, improbable
life I hold to my chest like a weapon. I know.
I know. This wasn't supposed to be about them.
You make me inordinately beautiful. Let's talk
about that. Or how I'm twelve years old & the cape
of a white durag billows from beneath my Marlins cap
like a sham poltergeist, flight & failure contained
within a single body, worthy core of any early
2000s-era New York rapper's coat of arms.
I was lying before. Once, while we sat, quiet
as mourners on the front porch, my father spat
that's a nice do you have there, eyeing the soft mess

of corkscrewed darkness atop his second-youngest
son's aging face, no sign of the good hair he praised
for years to family & coworkers alike. Alas, old friend,
you somehow make me even more opaque, make
me mystery, criminal, dope boy by the corner
of Broadway & 127th compelling respectable
women to reach for smartphones, call for backup.
My smooth, adjustable shadow. Like policy
or fire, you blacken everything you touch.

OWED TO THE HIGH-TOP FADE

You stand like a black-box theater in a one-pony town where no one likes theater. Except for the one pony. Who loves August Wilson. Especially the way August Wilson describes juba & inheritance & regret. I do not regret your genesis. I was simply unprepared for the side effects. How you announce my entrance for everyone on the subway car, how they fictionalize my vertical leap, my Spades telepathy, my court vision in overtime, you get what I'm getting at here. You're rocking the boat, my man! You grow out of this body in small black fists, like a poplar you could scale to heaven, like a shadow arguing for a body. You make this body unfamiliar. Mom & Dad loved you at first, but now you are three weeks past acceptable, an inch too long for adolescent phase, or interview, or the gravity of hard bristle & cocoa butter you refuse to obey. You refuse to obey. & I do not know how to care for anything or anyone that dares to break into this vault I built from scholarship money & easy praise, this armory skin. Teach me. Teach me to praise the flesh they flayed. My silhouette's gorgeous speed. The many contradictions of this name. You redeem.

OWED TO ANKLE WEIGHTS

Far as we could tell, Mark dreamt
of weightlessness & little else,
an entire career built upon

leapfrogging elephants
& lesser men. Though he
never deployed this exact

imagery in a public speech
or more casual tête-à-tête
over hot fries & Powerade,

the dream was well known
throughout the jailhouse
beige middle school hallways

we bolted through.
Mark wears ankle weights
every day because that

is what ballers do
when they are serious,
& Mark is very serious

when it comes to
the business of giving
out buckets as a kind

of spiritual practice, ascension
under control, an outlet
pass flying language-like

across the length
of the court, Mark
catching the so-worn

-it's-almost-gold
sphere in his dominant
palm, switching

to the left without what most
would call thought, soaring
like an invocation

to the cylinder & the crowd
leaps right along with him.
Hands aloft in awe

of the boy who must have
some falcon in his blood
-line somewhere, the sheer

eloquence of his movement
enough to make them forget
whatever heaviness like a second

skeleton held them flush to the ground
that day, whatever slight or malice
born in silence by necessity

simply melts, falls like a man
made of flowers to the floor.
When we closed our eyes

that year we all saw the same
fecund emptiness staring
back, imagined all we could

hammer our bodies into by way
of pure repetition: sprinting
to the bodega for Peanut Chews

before the cheese bus could leave
us behind, toting little
brothers all the way up

past the third flight
with no break for breath,
jumping rope with the girls by

the hydrant by the hardware
store at least once a week,
two-pound silver bricks

strapped to each leg,
tucked as if contraband
or some secret knowledge

into the lips of our lucky
socks, all that kept us
from drowning.

OWED TO THE CHEESE BUS

O, how we gave chase
on legs that bent like Air
-heads under front teeth
or early summer's graceless

gaze. The back seats that loved us
back. Our bodies flush
against their sticky green
leather glory once heat

was high enough for hydrants
to bloom: block boys molted
swagger, gathered laughing
to see red & yellow metal

croon cool. It was you
who taught uncute kids
the breaks, their hearts to flex
with pluck & pomp, re-spawn

when Valentine's Day cards
went unopened, when jewelry
stolen from Mom
& given to Melissa was worn

to homecoming with Jordan
who was an inch taller
than he should have been
& a mediocre chess player.

Who else could defang the shame
but you, great muse of Morlock
youth, patron saint
of the thirteen-yet-still-juice-box

-bearing multitudes?
Mom's Volvo? Quotidian
by comparison. They call you
yellow. I call you off-gold

chariot. Haven for homework
forgotten at home or forgone
altogether. Truth is, we all together
like this nowhere but here.

You wrought us. You drop us
off but never drop us. Even
when drivers threaten
to call the law,

or actually carry through
with such a pitiful joke
& we drop down for fear
of turning to smoke, you stay.

Your floors may be filthy, but they
are solid as a full life & we are young.
& quicksilver tongued. & learning
words like *inertia* for the first time.

PLURAL

You know I ain't scared to lose you.
—Nayvadius DeMun Wilburn aka Future

In the name of solidarity, I have given
myself over to the particular
fixations of my age: ducking
sleep, day-drinking
with my internet
friends, three or four
Instagram self-portraits
on the downtown A,
left arm angled high
enough to catch collarbone.
I'm learning how to participate
in the world. Why
just last week, I said *hello*
to a woman wearing a dress made of smoke
spilling Stella over both her hands
in a charming sort of way
as Trina offered a theory
of radical black self
-determination in the background
each line giving fresh velocity
to the room & yes I do
of course mean *that* Trina
whose unfettered praise
of the shaking of the booty
has always been
to my mind
a kind of talisman,
laic prayer lending valor
to the bashful & now
the woman in white
is talking to me
about the history of Liberia
& her favorite podcasts,

how good it feels
to see this many people dancing
in a city best known
for its casual indifference,
the impossible farness
between a mass of bodies
flush as paper sheaves
on the bus ride home,
six to an apartment built
for one, poverty & proximity
like two bladed halves
of the same long equation.
She types her number
into my right palm
& the boys go wild,
stain the floor
with handfuls of hyacinth
petals they cast
as if aspiration
into the soft
black air.
I'm pretty good
at not loving
anything enough
to fear its ruin.
The cruel speed
of our guaranteed
obsolescence suits
me. This way
I get to be at least one
of my favorite
versions of myself
every other week:
brooding philosopher,
race man, public apology
connoisseur, without
the pressure

of your seeing
where I keep
the parts I know
you would one day
wish I tucked away
or else killed
somewhere private
so you didn't
have to smell
the fire & all
I can think of
these days as I stare
across the table
past the drinks
with beautiful names
is how my friend Ibrahim
used to say *I'm not single,*
I'm plural & we all laughed
like we understood

PALIMPSESTINA

I spend my days studying the eloquent beast
juxtaposed against a given black
body living into its singular joy, i.e., forsythia
& lemonade in the middle of July, steel
pan playing loud enough to feel it. Hands
aloft in praise taken for surrender, left

then right, slowly. Nothing left
to an officer's imagination lest he manumit the beasts
which call his corners quarters, think his hands
tempest sent to scar the endless black
expanse. George Jackson bends steel
with every letter, & I can think only of the forsythia

growing in his lover's eyes, how *forsythia*
sounds like the name of a girl I knew before I left
town for hallways bereft of steel
-faced boys who named sorrow the beast
they slew daily, how they sustained a kind of black
humor about this business of being bound to one's hands

as conflict's only punctuation. Survival: how I lend my hands
to lyric's labor, as if forsythia
or chrysanthemum could bloom from black
ideas dancing across a screen. What is there left
to say about the dead space betwixt soul & beast,
the law as an eternal mouth, anxious for blood & steel?

Before I learned to steel
nerves in the face of a stranger's hands
swinging swift as a beast's
heart in chase or heat, my arms were forsythia
freshly grown, thinnest green, bad for business. Which left
only a world of fugitive black

letters to serve as my loophole of retreat, a black
wholeness to ease the wounds, flesh of gem & steel
to reflect the light of those who left
only faintest trace behind. May these hands
forever tend the soil of those songs, the forsythia
lives straining for air against the beast

-ly fear which seeks to calm the black steel beast
that sleeps within, the voice left praying *forsythia,
forsythia, make a world of these hands.*

THE OPEN

To be sure, there is a certain promiscuous relation
between what Rilke calls, in his eighth & greatest
elegy, *the open*, & what I meant in twelfth grade
when I dialed Tiana's digits into my aquamarine

Sprint flip phone, said *you free this Wednesday,
I got the open*, which was shorthand, of course,
for *open crib*, or *open house*, without the academic
associations that attend the latter phrase.

In Rilke's mouth, the term connotes a way
of seeing, the world as a blurring of body
& shape, no discernible split between
the water & its trout like broadswords

soft to the touch, lending their silver speed
to the landscape. I have spent years yearning
to be so close to the body of another
my mind might pass like mist from me,

an albatross I could shed without penance
or pain. Tiana leaves for the 64 bus
eventually, & I am only a boy
alone in his childhood bed, watching

the hours improve. At school the next
day, my friends adorn me
in their singular brutality, claim
Tiana has me *open*, outlined

in marigolds, my body luminous, my body
barely discernible, as if I had gazed
upon the edge of the known world
with all my eyes & yet lived

AMERICAN ABECEDARIAN

A is for atom bomb. B is for blacks belting blues before burial, the blood they let to give the flag its glimmer. C is for cocoon & its cognates. Cocaine, Coca-Cola, the cacophonous wail of drones filling air with wartime. D is for demagogue. E is for elephants & their semblances, every political animal laboring under some less-than-human name. F is for foxhole. Firefight. Fears we cathect onto men holding best intentions close to the chest as one might guilt or guns & of course G is for guns, G-men, guillotines draped in flame we dream any hellscape holds if it's up to snuff. H is for Horsepower. I is for *I*. I is for individual drive trumps all concern when it comes to this business of living joyously at the edge of wit, watching half a world drown with your hands tied. J is for jeans. K is for Krispy Kreme. L is for loss. L is for loveliness. L is for lean in the cups of boys in white shirts billowing free in Mississippi towns so small, they are visible only when passing through them, like death. M is for metafiction. N is for next: next wife, next car, next life I would spend the bones in this flesh one by one to touch. O is for opulence. Opportunity. Occasional anguish but nothing compared to what I will reach when I peak & P is for Preakness. Poverty & bodies that flee it. Oh body, like a storm of horses. Oh questions we dare not ask for fear of breaking rank or losing funding. Q is for quarantine. R is for repair, Revolution, other conflicts that lack limit in any definitional sense. S is for stars we adore & reflect. T is for tragedy. U is for upper-middle working class when the survey asks. V is for the viola my mother plays in the 1970s as her hometown collapses without fanfare. W is for Windows 98 in the public school computer lab & every fourth grader playing *Oregon Trail* there. X is for xanthan gum, every everyday ingredient you couldn't identify by sight if you tried. Y is for Yellowstone. Y is for the yachts in the docks in our eyes. Z is for zealotry: national pride like an infinite zip line, hyperdrive, the fastest way down.

TOKEN PLAYS THE DOZENS

Okay so boom I'm not that fast or strong but when it comes time to *go in* and/or *cut ass* as Chris & Omar call it I'm godlike. Slick. Every witticism swift as hearsay in pursuit though I'm barely even fresh-adjacent, e.g., my off-gold corduroys stay hermetically sealed to each flank, front teeth fanned in at least three directions, but that's the only joke anybody pretty got on me for real, that & my big head, which I can explain away anyhow, claim *but I don't even care 'cause my mama says that's where the imagination lives*, which goes over about as well as you might expect, though depending on the context I might pop back on some *Ya mama's so fat her belt line is the prime meridian Ya mama's so black she gets salt on her fingers and it looks like the universe Ya mama's so ugly when she walks into the corner store they turn the surveillance cameras off* & yes there are times this goes on for the entire lunch period, just me & my nonchalant cruelty up against a host of boys more beautiful than I & better dressed too, better loved both here & in the thick of the city once the D train releases us into the block's gray embrace & I am forced to pay for what I misread as the basic order of things, our mutual exchange of violences passed down clean as color or temperament, the blades between each molar honed at home watching my mother use her most luxurious words to pummel the man she loved into powder.

METAL POEM

is how Baraka described John Tchicai's deploying the horn
like a kind of war machine before either man's lungs were left empty
as a shipwreck, bodies still, stoic as stone & buried deep. Mainstream pop
had not yet given John his proper shine,
& so I sometimes like to think of the phrase as a chamber
with no flash or flame to kill the dim, so black it's blank, the lead

-off to some broader claim about what touch compels, or unmakes. Any leader
-less man will cut holes in the world if you let him breathe, I think. Every horn
holds a history of violence. Animals slain for the sake of sound. Chamber
music born of plundered bone. My entire block is metal poem. Endless empty
school desks mourned by shoes hung from telephone wire, so high they catch the shine
of dawn before anything living. & the beat goes on. Staccato pop

of steel a call to pray. Bloodstained denouement. Pop
hears the family car backfire & dreams of Vietnam, lead
spray autographing his left side from boot to hip. Sundays, he loved to shine
our shoes & skin until both glowed like opal. Sharp as a horn
-bill's kiss, my daddy was, before the weight of an empty
ledger winnowed him, left his chest hollow as the chamber

of a gun in the hands of a man six bodies deep into his rage, every chamber
of his tome-thick heart falling slack. The day it all went dark, Pop
barely spoke for more than a few clicks of the clock's one good hand. Empty
quiet, where once was laughter so full, we felt when it fell to the floor. *Who will lead
or love us now?* the people thought, when Moses melted that metal god from horn
to hoof, made them drink. For weeks, their insides shine

with the light of the fallen. Little novae. Little faiths aflame. O, how I wished to shine
the way Pop did when it came time for penance; my mother's stare, a chamber
of horrors, pulling names from him till they lie like fresh kill on our kitchen table, hornets
filling corpses with chatter. Every morning, the same perverse pop
quiz: *where have you been?* He responds as any weapon might. Leaden
expression to quell her pursuit. Either hand empty

apart from the car keys he will use to open the air between us again, empty
out our unearned dreams. His love for the idea of us never fails to shine
through. But for how long can you ask a man to lead
a life he never yearned for? Silence each chamber
clicking inside of him, coaxing both feet forward, demanding he pop
his son in the mouth for calling him *phantom* when he means to say *my heart is a horn*

in a hole in the earth is an empty cell cleansed of sunshine is a dead man's chamber
nothing worth dying for inside of it is a lead balloon is a prop
gun in a time of war is a single splintered thorn

STILL LIFE WITH TOY GUN

for Tamir Rice and John Crawford III

After the after-party empties both of its fists
the seven of us gather like a murder
of crows to loose bread around the last

table the dining hall has left. It's late,
& vegetarian pizza is the best thing
the joint has going, but we stay, mostly

to partake in what we would never call
gossip in front of our uncles but most
certainly is: who left with how many

numbers, top ten worst life choices
made that weekend, how Lauryn's cobalt
dress lassoed every human breath in the room.

Night unspools. Our attention plants
its feet in late Clinton-era Everywhere
& we sing of what we yearned for back then,

back home, what mocked our small,
stupefied hands like a white stove
or the promise of beauty.

Consensus lands on Super Soakers.
BB guns. All manner of false weaponry
we were barred from as boys

because of a mother's fear, her suspicion
that the rules of a given game might shift
& gunfire would be our only warning,

the policeman's voice an aftershock, his first mouth
having already made its claim. Even now, no one
among us calls this a kind of theft, which is to say,

the term never launches like a hex from our tongues,
but even if it did, somehow, rise & alight the air, if everything
we missed during the years we grew tired trying not to die

found its own body right then, right there in the center

of campus, what difference could it make now
that we have already mastered the rule book, the protocol

we learned before we learned to slow
dance, or smooth talk, or scream
the lyrics of a favorite song in a group

of two or more & not feel ashamed
of all the noise a black body can make
while it is still living

WHEN THY KING WAS A BOY

with thanks to Ed Roberson

The most recent headline on the Dead
      -spin front page reads *LeBron James*

is omnipotent & the first thing
      I think is that even back in 2006,

his advent means a certain kind of undeniable,
      post-soul apocalypse. The man

was low-key Copernicus
      in this sense, at least for all those boys

at the baseline of my memory's best
      eye, coming of age in M.J.'s wake,

wandering wild with no martyr
      to call archetype, no popular afterlife

through which to measure the value
      of a solitary human breath. We were sixteen

on the bench, starving for exits
      our bodies might build from hours spent

in tepid gyms & backs of buses
      scanning Faulkner, hedging our bets

with the books in case Cornell never called
      on the ball front, & we were forced to let go

of dreams already long-destroyed
      by genes & childhood vice. All that untapped

fleshly potential, sacrificed
        in the name of first-person shooters,

chess lessons, friends who fled
        when beatdowns swelled beyond

their means. But Bron would never
        do us like that. This we knew from his high

-definition entry into the land
        of the generally despised & perpetually syndicated,

only a year or so older than us but boundless
        in his vision & grace, vicious with the first step,

every outlet pass launching across
        the length of the court as if cannoned,

or indwelt by a god of pitch,
        summer waging its two-front war

on our hair & skin & no one
        cares to breathe. The boy king

rises like an aria. We sing.
        He, who will one day

carry entire economies
        in his stead, but for now

is little more than a hunter
        -green headband, honey

-colored 23 emblazoned
        across his chest like the chosen

few of us back then
     with the game or gall

to claim that we too
     had inherited the air.

MIKE BROWN IS A TYPE OF CHRIST

By which I mean, mostly, that we gaze upon the boy
& all of our fallen return to us, their wounds unhealed
& howling. I want to say something about *indeterminacy*
here. Decomposition as a kind of writing.
How the body never vanishes, really,
merely sketches the landscape anew
underground, foxgloves & marigolds jutting
like scimitars from the field's flesh,
precious weapons of those thought to be rot
already, soil's song, long gone past the grave.
For who says the dead don't think, don't shake
the weight of marrow & slip, quiet as fire, back
into whatever partition binds this life
to its grand black Epilogue? Last night,
I imagined every officer's gun
gathered & stuffed in a bombproof box
by the side of the highway; wondered
what they might choose to craft
with their hands, their eyes, both given
for so long to the work of chasing
what can't be contained. I dreamt unkillable
multitudes assembled in the wake
of a slain friend, the name
his mother once cast
like a cloak over him
the small & common blade
beneath their tongues

YOU ARE SO ARTICULATE WITH YOUR HANDS

she says & it's the first time
the word doesn't hurt. I respond
by citing something age-inappropriate
from Aristotle, drawing mostly
from his idea that hands are what make us
human, every gesture the embodiment
of our desire for invention or care, & I'm not
sure about that last part but it seemed
like a polite response at the time
& I'm not accustomed to not needing
to fight. If my hands speak with conviction
then blame my stupid mouth for its lack
of weaponry or sweetness. I clap when I'm angry
because it's the best way to get the heat out.
Pop says that my words are bigger
than my mouth, but these hands
can block a punch, build a bookcase,
feed a child & when's the last time
you saw a song do that?

OWED TO THE 99 CENT STORE

You are a kind of utopia,
you know. God's garage.
Counter-hegemonic

magic, how you tug
on a dollar bill
until it becomes an open

field, how you mock semiotics,
offering products which often
belie your professed mission,

your wondrous intentions,
all these too-expensive toasters,
fragile dishes, ironing boards

that make Mom appeal to American
Express as backup, her escape
route from unplanned shame.

You ain't have to do us like that.
But I peeped game. I know you
just like everyone else, hoping

to hustle your way off
this ziggurat block, all these
poor folks stacked on top

of one another like tropes.
Your true currency
is the cheer of children,

the love of learners
under duress, black & white
notebooks I still call upon

in hopes that these,
my most harried dreams,
might have rest, shelter

when smartphones give in,
fading to moonless wan
like everything else

around here. You persist.
You tenacious meditation
on excess. You candy bars

& batteries when pilot
lights kissed us no more
& Swedish Fish

were the best high we knew
or could afford.
You smorgasbord.

You sweet ecology.
You philosophy of boys
that have not yet learned

the wiring of value.
You neon name.
You anti-nihilism.

You clarion call
to the righteous
singing *come fill*

& be filled.

OWED TO THE PLASTIC ON YOUR GRANDMOTHER'S COUCH

Which could almost be said
to *glisten*, or glow,
like the weaponry
in heaven.
Frictionless.
As if slickened
with some Pentecost
-al auntie's last bottle
of anointing oil, an ark
of no covenant
one might easily name,
apart from the promise
to preserve all small
& distinctly mortal forms
of loveliness
that any elder
African American
woman makes
the day they see sixty.
Consider the garden
of collards & heirloom
tomatoes only,
her long, single braid
streaked with gray
like a gathering
of weather,
the child popped
in church for not
sitting still, how even that,
they say, can become an omen
if you aren't careful,
if you don't act like you know
all Newton's laws
don't apply to us
the same exactly.

Ain't no equal
& opposite reaction
to the everyday brawl
blackness in America is,
no body so beloved
it cannot be destroyed.
So we hold on to what
we cannot hold.
Adorn it
in Vaseline, or gold,
or polyurethane wrapping.
Call it ours
& don't
mean owned.
Call it just
like new,
mean *alive*.

REPARATION

Forty acres & a jewel-encrusted orchid crown
for each & every living baby girl

growing up the way
we did. The way

we do. Unbridled. Unburied
though we stay pursued

by the U.S. school-to-prison
state's laserlike vision.

Biweekly standing ovations.
Bras-Coupé resuscitated

with a sledgehammer slung over
his left shoulder, eyes ablaze

& dead set on the private
sector, the price

of four-year tuition, four-year
fascist presidents, any & all forms

of predatory opulence. Scholarships.
Scholars that love us

enough to break this language
lengthwise, filled as it is

with the bones of our fallen. Monuments
to the fallen. A grave site

for the illustrious Negro dead,
like Zora Neale Hurston said,

illustrious meaning you were black
& full of adoration, or vexed,

which is just another way
of saying you wanted to survive,

the world said die,
& you refused its refusal.

Another approach to the general
sentiment that Blackness

is beautiful, with no referent
to their everyday negation

of our essential, human splendor.
An apology on the Senate

floor. For the trade, the plunder
of our names, unremarked

graves, a hand in the hair,
a boot to the throat, guns

in the schools & the guns
are the books, the stares

of the second-grade teacher
calling your son a distraction,

your daughter's braids *illegal*,
your building a blight

on the neighborhood,
the good you do & dream

of never quite good
enough to merit

the bull's-eye's removal.
A ship to wherever

we point on a map
of the measurable

universe, dare call
harbor, sanctum, ground

where the children can play
& come home whole.

REPARATION

They tell you the tumor, at present,
is roughly four inches wide.

A manageable distance. One that you scale
with your hands, for some reason,
on the long ride back to Boston,
rather counterintuitively, as you were
trying to use them
to write something meaningful
about all this pain
the miniature killer inside
your father carved into you.

The gesture teaches you
absolutely nothing
about the space
between his inconstant body
& the dark man you chase
in all of your thinking.

He is hundreds of miles
away right now, probably,
sitting in a chair, staring
at the wall like a former assailant.

He is sending you text messages
with critical pieces of language
missing.

You grasp at the shards,
stupidly.

Little builder. Little mirror. Little body
-guard, throwing punches
at the flood.

REPARATION

How are you feeling? is always your opening question
& you know me. I invariably take it the wrong way
when you say it like that.

I hear you asking for damage reports, the autobiography
of this pile of brown rubble bumbling on

about his father's beauty, this chasm splitting
the voice in his unkempt head & the one
which enters the realm of the living.

You are good to me, & this kindness, I think, is not reducible
to our plainly economic relation, the yellow carbon
receipt at the end of each session a reminder
that we aren't just girls
in the park catching up, estimating the cost
of our high school errors.

I never call you my *analyst*, because
that makes me sound like a body
of work, some extended meditation
approaching theory, if only asymptotically.

Anyways. I'm all right today. I remembered
to eat breakfast, & went for a run uptown.

I gave myself credit for trying to change.

Something in me awakened, today,
ready for liftoff. It sang.

REPARATION

So much has been said
about black men
& their mothers,

almost none of which
works for you & me
because I am less

your acolyte, or boyfriend,
than I am your twin brother
of a sort, counterfeit currency

moving through the world
on your behalf, making things
move. We duel

because you created me,
& sometimes cannot
bear the trace of yourself

I belt out
by being here.
Laughing with all

my teeth. Debating
minutiae. Stealing your high
-heeled purple pumps, the ones

you once kept next to your dresser
drawer, putting them on,
sauntering across the house

like a soloist. I was four.
You were furious. You
forgave me.

Forgive me. I fear
sometimes I am four men
at once, each one

bludgeoning the other
based on some long-held
misunderstanding.

You urge me
to take better care
of this wilting

frame. Drink
water. Pop a pair
of echinacea capsules

each day. Devote
my *thought life* (your phrase)
to higher planes.

But what modern-day
black son wasn't born
knowing how to pray?

Doesn't meditate
on the gun, the badge,
a lover's hand

against the face or neck
to jog his memory,
recall his preordained

place? Encaged, prostrate,
enraged, enamored, no space
to make the world

you saw in visions
& scriptures, no,
this isn't the future

you dreamt of, Ma,
but it is the war
for which

you gave me vestments,
the day I stepped
onto your front porch,

bloodstained & half-asleep.
You bade me return
to the street. Face the boys'

onslaught head-on, remind them
whose I was, the name I carry,
the true & living god giving it form.

I was born
with a job.
I will die

with one. We live
in a country
with no language

for what you are,
& I persist
for the sake

of your glory.

TOKEN COMES CLEAN

What I desired most was approachlessness,
enough fear to mark a sharp & ardent

wall between me & the broader social
sphere, think: semi-invisible

force field, think: aura light
umber like Bruce Leroy.

A beauty one might use to keep
a state-sanctioned grave

at bay, the distance
this darker body ought

to buy but doesn't.
If evolution were kind,

we would all be fireproof
by now. A shame, to be sure: this

brutal truth boomeranging back
& forth across America's oeuvre,

History stammering with blood
in its throat, blood on the books, blood

on the leaves, & what can you right
-fully call living now that the dead

have learned to dance so well?
Knife wounds in the global sky,

White god on my childhood mind
& you want to talk about *repair*

FREDERICK DOUGLASS IS DEAD

& might very well remain that way,
    despite the best attempts
of our present overlord to resurrect

him without a single living
    black mother's permission.
If he should come, & be recognized

as anything other than the muted whisper
    of a body interred, I wish his return
as some strange & ungovernable terror,

a ghost story turned live & direct ectoplasm
    without warning: Frederick in the White
House kitchens, Frederick in the faucets,

Frederick posted up at every corner
    of the Oval Office, shredding documents
invisibly, a blade in each of his eighteen

laser hands. *Go off,* his more radical undead
    colleagues will exclaim. *You better tell that man
to keep your name out his mouth.* But Frederick

Douglass doesn't say a thing. Not yet.
    He's waiting for you & me, my grandmother
says. Frederick Douglass is irrevocably dead,

& refuses to ride until we are ready. Until
    our prayers are knives or sheets of flame:
Hear us, O Beloved, Fugitive Saint: Defer

*the rain. Grant us the strength of a rage
    we can barely fathom. Make us
brave as the flock in the fist*

of a storm. Unmoor every melody
   they built from our screams. Steady
our dreams. Keep us warm.

OWED TO LONG JOHNS

I remember thinking *these are like skin for my skin*
& a truer thing to call black to boot
as my first pair were blacker even
than my nascent curls, which turned
brown whenever they would wrestle
the light. My father called you *thermals*,
which always brought to mind
radioactive weapons of one kind
or another, two nuclear physicists
using casual shorthand over coffee.
For ten years, under thrift store denim
& corduroys rubbed raw
by Ms. Blint's blue carpet,
I rock your soft scales
with minimal fuss, only twice or so
grumbling to Pop about how
you make me appear,
if not heavier per se then just,
well, *stuck* in all of my clothes, that this
is on the whole untenable
for a boy my age, no small
tragedy given these were formative
years, you see, *critical* even
as it pertained to the glowing,
affirmative sense of my body
I would need for success
in the general public
situation. Pop's concern
remained with the cold,
& I remained a boy
cocooned, fed up, hungry
for better methods of breaking
winter's callous rule. Anything
other than having to leave
the oven door open, setting

my mother's best four black pots
to boil at once, our entire family
gathered as if shrapnel in the living
room, so close our bodies grew almost
indeterminate there, huddled like stars
under blankets to thaw

OWED TO YOUR FATHER'S GOLD CHAIN

Since we are already on the topic,
I casually mention that I think we should
name the baby *Ajax* & you laugh
so hard that both your shoulders shake

as you mouth an adamant no,
your arms waving wild in front
of your face like some novice
air traffic controller. You later explain

that this is not only quote unquote
a terrible name but also that it makes
you think of innumerable Thursdays
spent cleaning bathrooms at your grandma's

house. And yes, I know, there must be a joke
about class stratification in there somewhere,
since the name Ajax also makes me think
of that magical white dust in the cardboard

blue box long before it does any ancient
Greek demigod, but I tend to assume
my first thought is not my best thought,
as you now know well. I often attribute

this fact to my sound colonial education,
but am not yet sure what you would call
or think of it. One might say that this,
in fact, is a working definition for love

in a time of general disenchantment. The meticulous
consideration of all that slipped through
the mind's wet meshwork before, minor
miracles, like the number of bones in a human

hand. How yours unfastens like a memory
when I request an impromptu waltz
across the bar's threshold & we circle
one another, as if swordsmen, in the low light.

How the next week, you clasp your father's gold
chain at the back of my neck, call me beautiful
in your inside voice, barely breaking a whisper,
as if you can't hear the dawn roaring

its way through the bedroom window
just to catch a glimpse of us here,
barely mortal, shimmering at the cusp
of this strange & untamable world.

SUMMER JOB

For all we knew, there was no such thing as wealth
management internships sponsored by a father's
Harvard roommate, or else some Fifth Avenue gig
running iced coffee for fashionistas an hour's ride away
from where we stood, the darkest thing for miles,

trash collection claws extending from our sleeves
like some late eighties cyborg fantasy. We were bored
out of our brains, unlettered, sharp enough still
to know our place in the grander proletarian scheme:
a pair of scholarship kids paid to maintain campus

while our peers tried their hands at college physics,
American industry, psychedelics and road trips
to the Midwest with friends, all while Devin and I
stood in our standard-issue jumpsuits, adding another
coat of white paint to cafeteria walls without irony.

There were no small iron gods in our pockets then;
no machines to thread us into the invisible world, and so
we passed entire mornings listening to the ceremonies
of birds we couldn't name as we traversed the sides
of the highway, each step perfecting our soon-to-be

-flawless technique, dodging carrion, dividing paper waste
from condoms and bottles of Coors, just the way Jay taught
us our first day on call. I spent most breaks in the rift
between observation and dreams, pulling music from the filthy
tales each older man on the maintenance crew cast like a cure

into the mind of the other. Folklore filling the desolate
lecture halls where we took lunch, laughing as we traded
one tradition for another. No future worth claiming apart
from that broken boiler in the next building, blackbirds
trapped in the gutter-way, getting pipes fixed before fall.

ELEGY FOR THE MODERN SCHOOL

This much I can prove:
we were black & unfinished
in the Harlem of old,

a mass of naps
& Vaselined knees
before the promise

of faster Wi-Fi & craft
beer was code for
what it is code for.

& my mother would
drop us off in her '89
Toyota Camry, its cool

steel flesh the color of a
half-dead rhododendron.
& my big sister would hold on

to my left hand—which fit
in hers like a quarter's worth
of Peanut Chews back then

—until the bell bid us scatter.
I was a good boy, & thus
defined by a certain lust

for solitude, the countless
ways I learned to scream
don't touch. This was all I knew

of the world I had yet to name,
its utter indifference, its
physical laws, my sister

a kind of atmosphere,
more god or feeling
than another small,

finite body like mine
that could be known
well, or else unmade.

Miss Cherry owned a ruler
long as my daddy's
entire forearm,

called it *Redeemer*, kept
the instrument at the front
of our classroom

so as to enrich
our already budding
sense of the apocalyptic,

would rap our knuckles
& backsides with it
like a blacksmith in love

with his labor any time
we dared behave as if
we were, in her words,

*outside our natural
minds*. Our parents
thought this little more

than rational extension
of the age-old wisdom
when it comes to rearing

the hunted: *I cannot keep you*
alive, but will see you die
at my hands long before

the day I let the law erase
your name from the ledger
of the living. & so it was,

that in songs & parables
long-given to the tide
of Reagan & concrete

bleeding blackness
all over & wayward
shots meant

for men themselves too young
to know the scent of cells
& aspiration rotted through,

we learned how we arrived
at the underside of modernity,
children only while we were held

& honed within those broad
brick walls, a place for us
to be unburied & yet unashamed,

unassailable, unaware
of an entire order lingering
like lions at the door.

ELEGY FOR THE POLICE STATE

What I imagined first were pruning hooks.

Something biblical, agrarian, a new use
for metal once good for little
more than tearing the air
from a docile body. Then, a gesture
toward the speculative: improbable,
overdue machines, teleportation
pads & twelve-speed hover-bikes,
lightsabers that can't kill, but make you feel
warm & amorphous upon contact, like good
ramen, or when you find someone
else's money on the floor.

The exercise grew unwieldy,
so I gave my energies over
to more practical matters.
Who to call when you get robbed
or hit with a bat. Who else to feed the dogs
of entropy & personal choice, the price
we pay to live decent, which
is to say, far from the stench
of the dead & the dying interlocked,
unintelligible with all that gold
in their mouths.

Here's a story: once, freshly cast
by my old man to the hotel room wall,
throat now full of my own, unoriginal
blood, I knew I needed my father
dead, assumed the quickest route
would be to call the law. Twelve years old
& already this kind of contract killer,
I took my cue from scenes
at school, black wands buzzing

before each child marking us
ready for class or cuffs, no middle
ground to be found, really, what I have
since heard called a *pipeline* more of a smooth
continuum from hold to hold, everywhere
batons & threats of premature interment, everywhere
taupe walls like the ones in jail & someone's grandbaby
pummeled raw.

PURPLE CITY BYRD GANG

My lavender tee is tall
as a ballroom gown
but no one dares

to say anything like that
to my face. Durag bisected
by black & Carolina-blue

stitching to contrast,
each of my newly purchased
Air Force Ones

shimmering white
as opportunity.
Against the pull

of crass familiarity,
& my parents' warnings
about the historical

dangers of the D train,
I am posted up
on the Lower East Side,

dead set on buying
my first album without
supervision or shame.

The front cover reads
From Me to U & it almost
feels like a form

of direct address.
Me & Juelz Santana
are damn near the same

age & although I have yet
to hold a gun or serve
the block my will

is good. I am fifteen
& everything
is possible.

I am private school
by way of two buses,
one regional train,

a first alarm
at 5:25 a.m. shaking
the entire house

by its neck. My parents
know Jesus loves us
all, abhors

our weaknesses. Dip
-set is contraband
by extension.

Hence, I fled
to the basement
for cover, anxious

to hear a certain version
of my own moderate life
recited back to me

in spectacular hues,
Jacuzzis & bulletproof
vests, rhyming couplets

that all end in the exact
same word. Almost
as if some argument

for love beyond
magnetism. Some
postmodern parlor

trick. Some living, future
English, & everyone in it
is immortal.

THE PANTHER IS A VIRTUAL ANIMAL

with a line from Tavia Nyong'o

Anything that wants to be can be a panther. The black lion
or ocelot, the black cheetah or cornrowed uptown girl sprinting
down her neighborhood block just like one, in dogged pursuit
of the future world. In this frame, I imagine Huey and Bobby
as boys in the sense of gender and genre alike, an unbroken
line reading: *my life is an armor for the other*. Before black berets
or free breakfasts, then, there is friendship. Before gun laws
shifting in the wake of organized strength, leather jackets
shimmering like gypsum in the Northern California twilight—
or else magazine covers running the world over, compelling
everyday ordinary people across the spectrum of context
or color to sing *who wants to be a panther ought to be he can be it*
—there is love. The panther is a virtual animal. The panther
strikes only when it has been assailed. The panther is a human
vision, interminable refusal, our common call to adore ourselves
as what we are and live and die on terms we fashioned from the earth
like this. Our precious metal metonym. Our style of fire and stone.

ELEGY FOR PRISON

Without fail, at least one
student replies *but what will we do*

with all the murderers?
& the answer hasn't changed

since I first felt cuffs, read
Etheridge or Dwayne, heard

iron doors too heavy to dent
with any human

pair of hands thud shut.
We cannot speak

as if the killers are not
already among us, mowing

the lawn, getting promotions,
trying on their fresh winter coats.

As if my older brother were perpetual
-ly dressed for the role

of corner store stickup boy,
eyes preordained for making

out unmarked cop cars
from a distance,

calm as Jimmy Carter
while a handgun rests

below the pitch
-navy Avirex jeans Mama

got him to celebrate
high honor roll,

A's across the board, even
in Environmental Science,

where he struggled early on.
I get the argument.

Close the jails & there he goes
again, classic Shaun,

up at seven a.m. mapping out
ever more intricate ways

to rob grocery stores. Shaun
with the shotgun, Shaun

with the bullet
-proof skin, Shaun

with the stains on his blood.
No one comes out & says

he was born with them.
No one calls him a thug

or an emptiness, nothing
so gauche as all that, most

of those assembled
in the lecture hall

opt instead for terms
like *practical* or *natural*

selection say *let's be realistic*
here it's really a matter

of public order
I mean we have to

keep them all
somewhere right

if someone killed
my mother money

wouldn't help at all
I would want

to take away
the one thing they

can't ever take back
& that's *time*

THE NEXT BLACK NATIONAL ANTHEM

Will naturally begin
with a blues note.

Some well-adorned
lovelorn lyric

about how
your baby left

& all you got
in the divorce

was remorse.
& a mortgage.

& a somewhat
morbid, though

mostly metaphorical,
obsession with

the underground.
With how it feels

to live in such unrelenting
emptiness, unseen,

altogether un-correctable
by the State's endless

arms. Just imagine:
Ellison's Prologue

set to the most elaborate
Metro Boomin instrumental

you can fathom, brass
horns & pulsar cannons

firing in tandem
as Aretha lines a hymn

in the footnotes. Twelve
& a half minutes

of unchecked, bass-laden
braggadocio. An owed

to the unwanted.
The most imitated,

incarcerated human
beings in the history

of the world & every
nanosecond of the band's

boundless song belongs
to us. It is ours, the way

the word *overcome*
or *The Wiz* or Herman

Melville is ours. In every
corner store & court

of law. Any barbershop
argument or hours-long

spat over Spades. The Next
Black National Anthem

will, by the rule, begin
in blood, & span

our centuries-long war
against oblivion, elaborate

the anguish at the core
of our gentleness. How

that generosity is a kind
of weapon.

This music, a blade
-d criticism of a country

obsessed with owning
everything that shimmers,

or moves with a destination
in mind. Even the sky.

Even the darkness
behind our eyes

when we dream.

AMERICA WILL BE

after Langston Hughes

I am now at the age where my father calls me brother
when we say goodbye. *Take care of yourself, brother,*
he whispers a half beat before we hang up the phone,
& it is as if some great bridge has unfolded over the air
between us. He is sixty-eight years old. He was born in the throat
of Jim Crow Alabama, one of ten children, their bodies side
by side in the kitchen each morning like a pair of hands
exalting. Over breakfast, I ask him to tell me the hardest thing
about going to school back then, expecting some history
I have already memorized. Boycotts & attack dogs, fire
hoses, Bull Connor in his personal tank, candy paint
shining white as a slaver's ghost. He says: *Having to read*
The Canterbury Tales. He says: *Eating lunch alone.* Now, I hear
the word *America* & think first of my father's loneliness,
the hands holding the pens that stabbed him as he walked
through the hallway, unclenched palms settling
onto a wooden desk, taking notes, trying to pretend
the shame didn't feel like an inheritance. You say *democracy*
& I see the men holding documents that sent him off
to war a year later, Motown blaring from a country
boy's bunker as napalm scarred the sky into jigsaw
patterns, his eyes open wide as the blooming blue
heart of the light bulb in a Crown Heights basement where he
& my mother will dance for the first time, their bodies
swaying like rockets in the impossible dark & yes I know
that this is more than likely not what you mean
when you sing *liberty* but it is the only kind
I know or can readily claim, the times where those hunted
by history are underground & somehow daring to love
what they cannot hold or fully fathom when the stranger
is not a threat but the promise of a different ending
I woke up this morning & there were men on television
lauding a wall big enough to box out an entire world,
families torn with the stroke of a pen, the right to live

little more than a garment that can be stolen or reduced
to cinder at a tyrant's whim my father knows this grew up
knowing this witnessed firsthand the firebombs
the Klan multiple messiahs love-soaked & shot through
somehow still believes in this grand bloodstained
experiment still votes still prays that his children might
make a life unlike any he has ever seen. He looks
at me like the promise of another cosmos & I never
know what to tell him. All of the books in my head
have made me cynical & distant, but there's a choir
in him that calls me forward my disbelief built as it is
from the bricks of his belief not in any America
you might see on network news or hear heralded
before a football game but in the quiet
power of Sam Cooke singing that he was born
by a river that remains unnamed that he runs
alongside to this day, some vast & future country
some nation within a nation, black as candor,
loud as the sound of my father's
unfettered laughter over cheese eggs & coffee
his eyes shut tight as armories his fists
unclenched as if he were invincible

Poet, performer, and scholar Joshua Bennett is the author of *The Sobbing School*. He received his PhD in English from Princeton University, and is currently Mellon Assistant Professor of English and Creative Writing at Dartmouth College. His writing has been published in *The New York Times Magazine*, *The Paris Review*, *Poetry*, and elsewhere. His book *Being Property Once Myself: Blackness and the End of Man* was published by Harvard University Press in May 2020. His first work of narrative nonfiction, *Spoken Word: A Cultural History*, is forthcoming from Knopf. He lives in Boston.

GAROUS ABDOLMALEKIAN
Lean Against This Late Hour

PAIGE ACKERSON-KIELY
Dolefully, A Rampart Stands

JOHN ASHBERY
Selected Poems
*Self-Portrait in a Convex
   Mirror*

PAUL BEATTY
Joker, Joker, Deuce

JOSHUA BENNETT
Owed
The Sobbing School

TED BERRIGAN
The Sonnets

LAUREN BERRY
The Lifting Dress

JOE BONOMO
Installations

PHILIP BOOTH
*Lifelines: Selected Poems
   1950–1999*
Selves

JIM CARROLL
*Fear of Dreaming: The
   Selected Poems*
Living at the Movies
Void of Course

ALISON HAWTHORNE
DEMING
Genius Loci
Rope
Stairway to Heaven

CARL DENNIS
Another Reason
Callings
*New and Selected Poems
   1974–2004*
Night School
Practical Gods
Ranking the Wishes
Unknown Friends

DIANE DI PRIMA
Loba

STUART DISCHELL
Backwards Days
Dig Safe

STEPHEN DOBYNS
*Velocities: New and Selected
   Poems: 1966–1992*

EDWARD DORN
Way More West

HEID E. ERDRICH
Little Big Bullys

ROGER FANNING
The Middle Ages

ADAM FOULDS
*The Broken Word: An Epic
   Poem of the British Empire
   in Kenya, and the Mau Mau
   Uprising Against It*

CARRIE FOUNTAIN
Burn Lake
Instant Winner

AMY GERSTLER
Dearest Creature
Ghost Girl
Medicine
Nerve Storm
Scattered at Sea

EUGENE GLORIA
*Drivers at the Short-Time
   Motel*
Hoodlum Birds
My Favorite Warlord
Sightseer in This Killing City

DEBORA GREGER
By Herself
*Desert Fathers, Uranium
   Daughters*
God
In Darwin's Room
Men, Women, and Ghosts
Western Art

TERRANCE HAYES
*American Sonnets for My Past
   and Future Assassin*
Hip Logic
How to Be Drawn
Lighthead
Wind in a Box

NATHAN HOKS
The Narrow Circle

ROBERT HUNTER
Sentinel and Other Poems

MARY KARR
Viper Rum

WILLIAM KECKLER
Sanskrit of the Body

JACK KEROUAC
Book of Blues
Book of Haikus
Book of Sketches

JOANNA KLINK
Circadian
*Excerpts from a Secret
   Prophecy*
The Nightfields
Raptus

JOANNE KYGER
As Ever: Selected Poems

ANN LAUTERBACH
Hum
*If in Time: Selected Poems,
   1975–2000*
On a Stair
Or to Begin Again
Spell
Under the Sign

CORINNE LEE
Plenty
Pyx

PHILLIS LEVIN
May Day
Mercury
Mr. Memory & Other Poems

PATRICIA LOCKWOOD
Motherland Fatherland
  Homelandsexuals

WILLIAM LOGAN
Macbeth in Venice
Madame X
Rift of Light
Strange Flesh
The Whispering Gallery

J. MICHAEL MARTINEZ
Museum of the Americas

ADRIAN MATEJKA
The Big Smoke
Map to the Stars
Mixology

MICHAEL MCCLURE
Huge Dreams: San Francisco
  and Beat Poems

ROSE MCLARNEY
Forage
Its Day Being Gone

DAVID MELTZER
David's Copy: The Selected
  Poems of David Meltzer

ROBERT MORGAN
Dark Energy
Terroir

CAROL MUSKE-DUKES
Blue Rose
An Octave Above Thunder:
  New and Selected Poems
Red Trousseau
Twin Cities

ALICE NOTLEY
Certain Magical Acts
Culture of One
The Descent of Alette
Disobedience
For the Ride
In the Pines
Mysteries of Small Houses

WILLIE PERDOMO
The Crazy Bunch
The Essential Hits of Shorty
  Bon Bon

DANIEL POPPICK
Fear of Description

LIA PURPURA
It Shouldn't Have Been
  Beautiful

LAWRENCE RAAB
The History of Forgetting
Visible Signs: New and
  Selected Poems

BARBARA RAS
The Last Skin
One Hidden Stuff

MICHAEL ROBBINS
Alien vs. Predator
The Second Sex

PATTIANN ROGERS
Generations
Holy Heathen Rhapsody
Quickening Fields
Wayfare

SAM SAX
Madness

ROBYN SCHIFF
A Woman of Property

WILLIAM STOBB
Absentia
Nervous Systems

TRYFON TOLIDES
An Almost Pure Empty
  Walking

VINCENT TORO
Tertulia

SARAH VAP
Viability

ANNE WALDMAN
Gossamurmur
Kill or Cure
Manatee/Humanity
Trickster Feminism

JAMES WELCH
Riding the Earthboy 40

PHILIP WHALEN
Overtime: Selected Poems

ROBERT WRIGLEY
Anatomy of Melancholy and
  Other Poems
Beautiful Country
Box
Earthly Meditations: New and
  Selected Poems
Lives of the Animals
Reign of Snakes

MARK YAKICH
The Importance of Peeling
  Potatoes in Ukraine
Spiritual Exercises
Unrelated Individuals
  Forming a Group Waiting
  to Cross